Learn ITALIAN Through Fairy Tales

Cinderella

Book Design & Production: Slangman Kids *(a division of Slangman Inc. and Slangman Publishing)*

Copy Editor: Julie Bobrick
Illustrated by: "Migs!" Sandoval
Translator: Alessio Filippi
Proofreader: Valerio Morucci

Copyright © 2006 by David Burke

Published by: Slangman Kids *(a division of Slangman Inc. and Slangman Publishing)* 12206 Hillslope Street, Studio City, CA 91604 •USA • Toll Free Telephone from USA: 1-877-SLANGMAN (1-877-752-6462) • From outside the USA: 1-818-SLANGMAN (1-818-752-6462) • Worldwide Fax 1-413-647-1589 • Email: info@slangman.com • Website: www.slangman.com

"Migs!" Sandoval
✳ our illustrator ✳

Miguel *"Migs!"* Sandoval has been drawing cartoons since the age of 6 and has worked on numerous national commercials and movies as a sculptor, model builder, and illustrator. He was born in Los Angeles and was raised in a bilingual household, speaking English and Spanish. He currently lives in San Francisco where he is working on his new comic book series!

ISBN10: 1891888-773
ISBN13: 978189888-779
Printed in the U.S.A.

10 9 8 7 6 5 4 3 2 1

Order Form

Preview chapters & shop online!

www.slangman.com

SHIP TO: _____

_____

_____

_____

Contact/Phone/Email: _____

SHIPPING

Domestic Orders

SURFACE MAIL
(Delivery time 5-7 business days).
Add $5 shipping/handling for the first item, $1.50 for each additional item.

RUSH SERVICE
Available at extra charge. Contact us for details.

International Orders

SURFACE MAIL
(Delivery time 6-8 weeks).
Add $6 shipping/handling for the first item, $2 for each additional item. Note that shipping to some countries may be more expensive. Contact us for details.

AIRMAIL (approx. 3-5 business days)
Available at extra charge. Contact us for details.

Method of Payment (Check one):

☐ Personal Check or Money Order
(Must be in U.S. funds and drawn on a U.S. bank.)

☐ VISA ☐ Master Card ☐ Discover ☐ American Express ☐ JCB

Credit Card Number

_____ | | | |

Signature / Expiration Date

QTY	ISBN-13	TITLE	PRICE	LEVEL	TOTAL COST
English to CHINESE (Mandarin)					
	9781891888-793	Cinderella	$14.95	1	
	9781891888-854	Goldilocks	$14.95	2	
	9781891888-915	Beauty and the Beast	$14.95	3	
English to FRENCH					
	9781891888-755	Cinderella	$14.95	1	
	9781891888-816	Goldilocks	$14.95	2	
	9781891888-878	Beauty and the Beast	$14.95	3	
English to GERMAN					
	9781891888-762	Cinderella	$14.95	1	
	9781891888-830	Goldilocks	$14.95	2	
	9781891888-885	Beauty and the Beast	$14.95	3	
English to HEBREW					
	9781891888-922	Cinderella	$14.95	1	
	9781891888-939	Goldilocks	$14.95	2	
	9781891888-946	Beauty and the Beast	$14.95	3	
English to ITALIAN					
	9781891888-779	Cinderella	$14.95	1	
	9781891888-823	Goldilocks	$14.95	2	
	9781891888-892	Beauty and the Beast	$14.95	3	
English to JAPANESE					
	9781891888-786	Cinderella	$14.95	1	
	9781891888-847	Goldilocks	$14.95	2	
	9781891888-908	Beauty and the Beast	$14.95	3	
English to SPANISH					
	9781891888-748	Cinderella	$14.95	1	
	9781891888-809	Goldilocks	$14.95	2	
	9781891888-861	Beauty and the Beast	$14.95	3	
Japanese to ENGLISH 絵本で えいご を学ぼう					
	9781891888-038	Cinderella	$14.95	1	
	9781891888-045	Goldilocks	$14.95	2	
	9781891888-052	Beauty and the Beast	$14.95	3	
Korean to ENGLISH 동화를 통한 ENGLISH 배우기					
	9781891888-076	Cinderella	$14.95	1	
	9781891888-106	Goldilocks	$14.95	2	
	9781891888-113	Beauty and the Beast	$14.95	3	
Spanish to ENGLISH Aprende INGLÉS con cuentos de hadas					
	9781891888-953	Cinderella	$14.95	1	
	9781891888-960	Goldilocks	$14.95	2	
	9781891888-977	Beauty and the Beast	$14.95	3	

Total for Merchandise ____

Sales Tax *(California residents only add applicable sales tax)* ____

Shipping *(See left)* ____

ORDER GRAND TOTAL ____

Prices subject to change

(a division of Slangman Publishing)

**** TO PLACE AN ORDER - CALL, FAX, OR EMAIL: ****

Phone: 1-818-752-6462 • Fax: 1-413-647-1589
Email: info@slangman.com • Web: www.slangman.com
12206 Hillslope Street • Studio City, CA 91604

(FORM 07160)

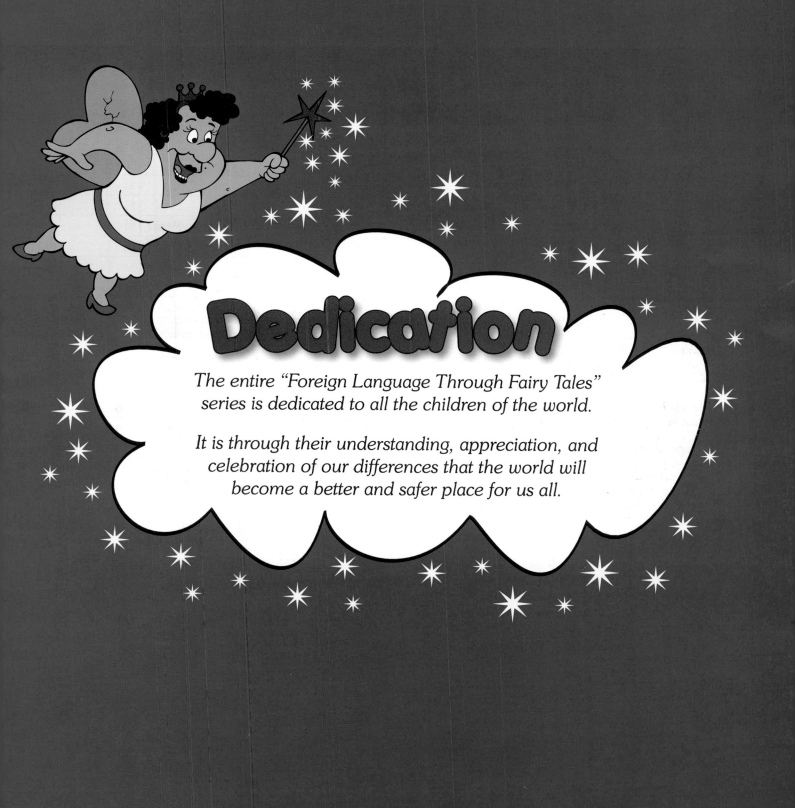

Dedication

The entire "Foreign Language Through Fairy Tales" series is dedicated to all the children of the world.

It is through their understanding, appreciation, and celebration of our differences that the world will become a better and safer place for us all.

1

ragazza

bella

Once upon a time, there lived a girl named Cinderella who was very pretty. The **bella ragazza** lived in a small

casa

house with her stepmother and two

stepsisters. At times it was difficult for the **bella ragazza** to live in such a small **casa** with her stepmother and stepsisters. Why? Because they were

3

cattiva ← jealous that she was so **bella** which is why her stepmother was extra mean to her. But the **bella ragazza** never complained about living in a small

casa with her stepmother who was
very **cattiva**, and two stepsisters, even
though they forced her to do all the work
in the entire **casa** day in and day out!

5

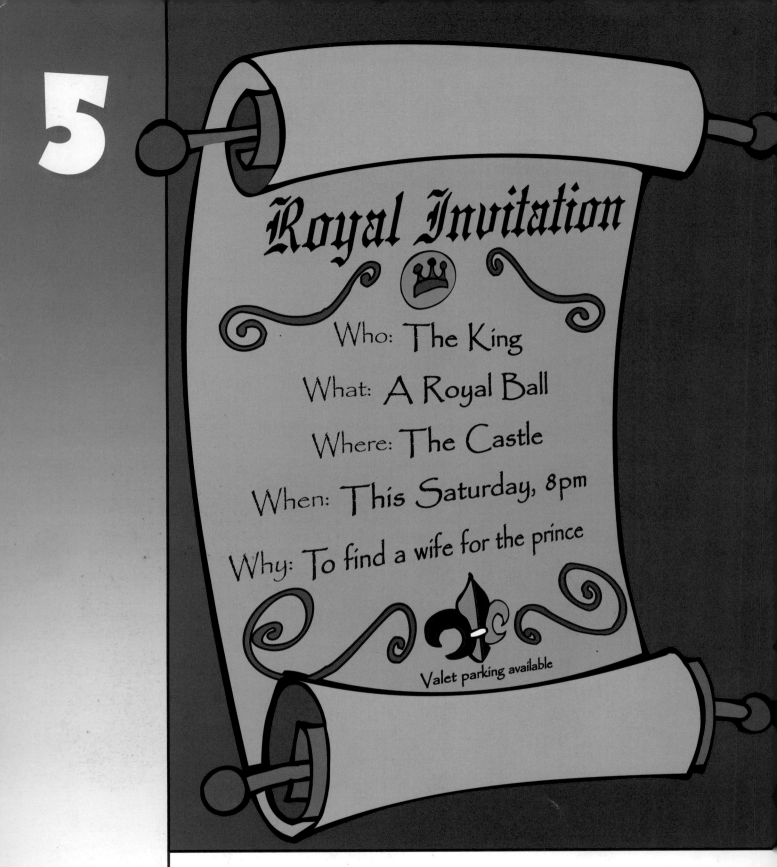

Royal Invitation

Who: The King

What: A Royal Ball

Where: The Castle

When: This Saturday, 8pm

Why: To find a wife for the prince

Valet parking available

One day, a royal invitation arrived at the **casa** of the **bella ragazza**. The king was throwing a (party) for the prince. And the **festa** was going to be (big).

festa

grande

A **grande festa**! The prince was very (handsome), not only **bello**, but kind. And every **ragazza** in the land was invited to the **grande festa** so that he could choose a (wife).

bello

moglie

7

principe ←

The king and queen also hoped the prince
would find a **moglie** who was truly **bella**
both inside and out. The **principe** was
very excited about the **grande festa**!

The night of the **grande festa** for the
principe arrived but Cinderella was [sad]. ➝ **triste**
Her stepmother was so **cattiva**, she wouldn't
let her leave the **casa** to go to the **festa**!

9

She was so **triste**, she started to cry. She was the only **ragazza** not allowed to leave her **casa** and get the chance to meet the **principe** at the **grande festa** and become his **moglie**.

Suddenly a voice from behind her said, "My dear, I'm your fairy godmother and you're going to the **grande festa** and you'll be wearing an elegant [dress]!"

vestito

Grazie ←

And with a wave of her wand, Cinderella was now wearing the most elegant **vestito** imaginable. "Thank you! **Grazie!**" exclaimed Cinderella. She

was a **bella ragazza** wearing an elegant **vestito**, and eager to leave her **casa** to meet the **principe** at the **grande festa** in hopes of becoming his **moglie**!

13

momento

mezzanotte

"One (moment)!" the fairy godmother added. "Make sure to leave the **grande festa** by (midnight) because your **vestito** will change back to the way it was!"

Cinderella thought for a **momento** then said, "I'll remember to leave before **mezzanotte**." So, the **bella ragazza** left for the **grande festa**. She was

15

The Royal FESTA

felice ←

no longer **triste**, but very [happy] to be meeting the **principe**. As she got out of her carriage, she could hear the **grande festa**! Cinderella walked in and

wasn't too **felice** to see more than one
bella ragazza waiting to meet the
principe. But after a **momento**,
she calmed down and was ready to

17

innamorato ◄

meet the **principe** face to face. And indeed he was **bello**! She could hardly believe her eyes! And clearly the **principe** was in love with the **bella ragazza**

the very first **momento** he saw her!

"**Grazie** for inviting me" said Cinderella.

"You're welcome" replied the **principe**.

"**Prego**!" They danced and danced for

Prego

hours, until the stroke of **mezzanotte** was upon them which the **bella ragazza** had completely forgotten about! *Poof!* Her **vestito** vanished!

Arrivederci

"Goodbye!" shouted Cinderella.
"**Arrivederci** and **grazie** for inviting
me!" "**Prego**," responded the **principe**.
And Cinderella ran back to her **casa**.

scarpa ←

The only thing she left behind was a glass shoe . The **principe** was extremely **triste** and went from town to town looking for a **bella ragazza** whose

foot would fit the glass **scarpa**. After days of eliminating **bella ragazza** after **bella ragazza**, the **principe** was very **triste** but he had one more **casa** to visit.

The **cattiva** stepmother and two stepsisters ran out to try on the glass **scarpa**. But the **principe** still couldn't find a **piede** to match the **scarpa**.

The **principe** was **triste** and about to give up, but at that very **momento**, he spotted Cinderella. There was something very special about her.

25

He just had to see if her **piede** was
the one that could fit the glass **scarpa**.
He knelt down in front of her and
slid the **scarpa** on her **piede**.

And her **piede** fit the glass **scarpa**
perfectly! At that very **momento**,
Cinderella's fairy godmother reappeared
and changed her back into the same

bella ragazza in the elegant **vestito** the **principe** had met at his **grande festa**. He was now more **innamorato** than ever! The **bella ragazza** was **felice**

that she lost her glass **scarpa** at the **grande festa** or the **principe** may never have found her! Soon, Cinderella became his **moglie** at a wedding that was far from

small. It was truly **grande**! She was so very **felice**! Cinderella would never be **triste** again. And the **principe** and Cinderella, lived in the castle happily ever after.